Actual Tigers

Poems

William Crawford

13547 Ventura Boulevard
Sherman Oaks CA 91423
eappublishing@gmail.com

www.EdgarAllanPoet.com

Actual Tigers
William Crawford © 2012

All Rights Reserved.

No part of this book may be used, reproduced, stored in a retrieval system or transmitted by any means whatsoever without written consent or permission from the publisher except for embodiment in brief quotations for the purpose of critical articles or reviews.

Actual Tigers
Poems
by William Crawford

Editing by Apryl Skies & Alicia Winski

ISBN -13: 978-0985471521
ISBN -10: 0985471522

Library of Congress Control Number:
2012949243

Printed in the United States of America

to
Sadie

*Out of the strong
came forth sweetness.*

Contents

Foreword	VII
Kneeling Poem's Plea	14
Why did you film clouds?	16
Recognizing the Fragile Before it Needs Fixing	18
Gravitas	21
Uncut Rain	22
Her Measurements	24
Arable	25
Bottom Sustenance	26
Righteous Epic(ene)	27
Measuring Cups	30
Actual Tigers	33
The Stoker	35
How I Disappear	39
Just a Shadow	41
The Noble Rise Above	43

Love does migrate this way, more so during summer	44
Country Bluebird Reimagined	46
Her blue ribbons, caught up in the breeze like that.	50
Photograph of Water	51
Felo de se	52
Her heavy hand	53
Specific Gravity	56
It doesn't take a professor.	59
Pantry Pride	60
Outlaw Banking	63
Frontier Doctored	64
Potatoes	67
Head On	69
Beguilement (or what Klaus said to the Butterfly)	71
Nearly a Morning	76
Watercolour of a Lighthouse	80
Blood on Blood	83
Staircase Wit	85

Blepharospasm	89
Anatomy of Egg	94
Sunspots	97
Neural Piano	100
Cancel Stars	105
May Day	111
In the Depths of Something Good	114
Acknowledgements	117
About the Author	118

Foreword

Actual Tigers by William Crawford is a thing of alchemy, more journey than tale. The poems of this collection have a unique pulse and purpose. The keen use of language, musicality and cinematic imagery is articulate and sophisticated, yet non pretentious. As an author, Crawford not only respects the reader, he respects his poems. This is clear from the unleashing of the first "tiger", in which he writes from the poem's perspective.

> You trapped me, you caged me,
> you raised me for pure slaughter value.
> Stuffed me with moon mad metaphor
> and red threadbare simile over easy.
> Slender means for your foie gras goose—
> a famine mistook for a feast.
> ~From *Kneeling Poem's Plea*

This piece is indeed, a feast for readers and a testament to the author's sagacity. While many writers force poetry into frame and call it art, Crawford's poems manifest intuitively and instinctively to the page with humble agenda and intent.

Do not mistake his metaphor for madness here, as an animal rights activist each word is embossed upon the reader for a reason. The use of "foie gras" in the above passage is an astute stance against animal cruelty in that the poem pleads for mercy from its writer.

Several ongoing themes will unfold in *Actual Tigers*, but the tenor cannot be articulated in a simple foreword. There is a sublime transfixion which occurs upon reading this tome.

How would one describe a sunset to someone who was not there to witness it? Even photographs will pale in vision and the photographer may miss the moment bringing the camera into focus.

> Then the pause
> where you showed me
> the space inside seconds—
> un-tethered from logic,
> from physics—
>
> weightless, again.
>
> I follow your instruction
> to prevent suspicious rust,
> avoiding the technology
> that dead-ends the soul.
> ~From *Why did you film clouds?*

In the above deeply meditative poem, Crawford expresses the indelible footprint humans can and should leave behind. The wisdom gained by listening and experiencing wholly each fleeting moment is preciously invaluable to the soul. This poem is simplistic in its obscurity, begging the questions we are often too assiduous to acknowledge or perhaps, too distracted to see when beauty is written in the sky.

Further expressed in this piece is with the philosophy in place that each moment is vital, nothing is ever lost; the indelible mark, the searing and often painful truth we are privileged enough to bear by existence alone.
Crawford's poems are wise enough to raise all the right questions, but mindful not to deliver all the answers.

> He has convinced himself
> that the question holds
> more weight
> than the answer,
>
> as he fashions a knife
> from poached ivory
> all blade
> no handle.
>
> He sees blood
> on his hands
> and feels proud.
> ~From *Gravitas*

In *Gravitas* there is also a strong element of activism in the use of language; an understated, yet profound message of compassion and responsibility.

Through the purity of vision present in his poetry, Crawford inspires readers to live by peaceful means and grander intention. The best example of this is in the signature poem;

> I just want another season,
>
> says the wounded tiger
> as he staggers back

> to the place he first
> found beauty
>
> starving
>
> seeking sustenance,
> shade, mate
>
> only to find paper
> where meat used to be
> ~From *Actual Tigers*

This passage is perhaps the most powerful and symbolic of the entire collection. The sublime metaphor of paper versus meat is thought-provoking and profoundly tragic demanding a "captured breath" from the reader.

Crawford's poetry is always honest and personal. In the following tribute poem the ability to weave metaphor and maintain a sense of familiarity and reflection is monumental.

> The dust asks the cleaning lady
> When the singer of songs is coming home
> And will the sky be following him
> You bet the birds are standing still
> ~From *Love does migrate this*
> *way, more so during summer*
> *- for Scott Wannberg*

Actual Tigers in its entirety is certainly not without hope. It is however, a lesson in humanity and humility. Still, the poet refrains from taking himself too seriously.

In poems such as *It doesn't take a professor* and *Pantry Pride* the author allows room for humor, a signature element for Crawford. While one is a refreshing dose of witticism, the other is colorful and character driven, both unique without losing sight of the bigger picture.

There is a fine balance and tearful quality to this artful collection. Many poems wash over the reader with intrinsic beauty and lexicon. In the following excerpt, Crawford shows a distinct tenderness which tease the senses in dreamy lines such as;

> when she returns to me
> with skin softened
> by lazy country days
> and lavender oil
> she'll read stories
> from memory
> faraway eyes
> indexing frontiers
> and I will listen
> still as a sleeping horse
> ~From *Her blue ribbons, caught up in the breeze like that.*
> *- for Kimberly Schlagel*

In closing, *Actual Tigers* is more than a book. William Crawford has brought to life something far more important than simply writing great poetry. As a storyteller his poems and the overall sentimentality of *Actual Tigers* unleashes in the reader something imperative and reminds us of the importance of living "*In the Depths of Something Good*" while we still have the chance.

by Apryl Skies

*"I knew there were, in myself, the souls
of millions of people who lived centuries ago;
not just people but animals, plants, the elements,
things, even matter. All of these exist in me."*

~Klaus Kinski

Kneeling Poem's Plea

I'm a living thing
created in your image
so please show some mercy.

Allow pause, a captured breath,
perhaps even a moment of release
before you start screaming at me,
wailing on me again.

You trapped me, you caged me,
you raised me for pure slaughter value.
Stuffed me with moon mad metaphor
and red threadbare simile over easy.
Slender means for your foie gras goose—
a famine mistook for a feast.

Quick, take the feeding hand,
stick the quill back in,
let it serve a greater purpose.

Pin me, dry mount me.
Leave me ripped and hanging in the raw air open.
A sick dangling spangle empty, bereft of light,
in your vainglorious den—
a trophy, I suppose.

I'm still alive!

The Muse (remember her?)
is here to mediate this.

We see you kneecapped—
a starved shape inside your confessional

lined and re-lined with stillborn sheets.

Used and abused, battered loyal,
we are standing here
above your razed cathedral
still willing to help you
lose yourself.

Why did you film clouds?

You see,
I never really lost you—

how does one lose sight of a torch
in this dark glacial age?

The fluid movement
of your new hypnotic—

then the pause
where you showed me
the space inside seconds—
un-tethered from logic,
from physics—

weightless, again.

I follow your instruction
to prevent suspicious rust,
avoiding the technology
that dead-ends the soul.

I find you when I close my eyes…
you rise and surround me—
it is here I find truth,
the key you promised.

In a dream we stretch
and merge on the pond's reflective skin.
Our thoughts become substance,
a common island—
a place of rest, a home.

Remember the time
I found you naked,
half-asleep, half-awake,
reaching for your reflection
in the mirror?

You said, "help me, I'm fading."
I opened my eyes, and said…

Recognizing the Fragile Before it Needs Fixing

he never really lost that look
of a kid caught in the Christmas lights

only back then
the null experience
the hook and ladder void
was unknown

the light had a different slant
bending without strain
to find him
laughing at his own thoughts

those days language wasn't
used as a weapon or defense mechanism–
a brackish moat surrounding lonely castle
filled with snapping turtles
slow surface of broken mirror and smoke

no– the words were Swiss allies
with chocolate watches
and tiny knives to cut cheese
he loved them
the peace they'd bring

sustaining him
like a good woman
that reminded him of mother

only now those lights
seemed empty between blinks

what was there to remember
beyond the words?

the open fields
with actual air secreted
inside green pockets
leaving only the heavy empty
to be breathed

the blackout valleys
and low bald hills
of the English tongue

those words
a weakness
a clumsy surgeon
whose work disfigured
the feeling

what could they possibly say
about this ripped dago red rhapsody
tangled up in the depth of his gut?

the blunt instruments
striking so many bells
in the guarded towers
of his endlessly tolling
restlessly toiling mind

give the tongue to the cat
let her try to explain it
she's smart enough to know better

he needed a new language
one without mask or trap

a sustenance that offered
enlightenment over obfuscation

he could hear it
he could feel it
changing inside

forming an honest buffer
more light than shield

no rise or fall
just quiet plateau

his exact thought:
how sweet silence sounds
no wonder it's a song.

Gravitas

Challenger is all gamble no spark
when he bets on night
with slender means.

He has convinced himself
that the question holds
more weight
than the answer,

as he fashions a knife
from poached ivory
all blade
no handle.

He sees blood
on his hands
and feels proud.

Day arrives
as expected;

every error
brighter now.

His blood
a half-baked cake
wishing to be candle;

all of this
friction without flame.

Uncut Rain
for Hart Crane

The night sleeps with thirty sailors
Stands slowly burning yet still
A broken tower without a bell
Without music to mark its own passing
As it falls with you, then within you.

You were always lost at sea
Forever drowning in your own depths.

An awkward bird of a man
Diving beak first into everything
If only to taste its decay
Describe the earthy notes
The aftertaste smacked of afterlife
It was eternally vernal,
Or did you say, *eternally infernal?*

So many eyes arresting you
As you danced drunken sarabandes
With your handsome sailor
Suited in moonlight flooding
Starboard side of the Orizaba
Two target range silhouettes becoming one
Fragments of filmy shot shadow mending.

Then the murderous sun of morning
Found floundering fledgling falling
And the words you mouthed failed
In the raw red meat face of day
The men it mothered and dressed
As lions in the most ignorant pride.

Hold a conch shell to each ear
Before you blow this reveille
In hopes that they will listen
To the earnest, imploring sound
Of blood in song, in sonnet,
Forever thinking it is the sea
Or just a photograph of water.

Shattering yourself in blue melody
Against shimmering sheets of uncut rain
With an unctuous tongue full of the gulf's sweat
Climbing down through cerulean chambers
While still facing the raging surface

Where the sun's truth
Is just a broken yolk
Or maybe only a golden eye
With which to see yourself reflected
In the cold fathomless water below
Crossing another bridge as it burns.

Listening all the while
For the gentle pity of laughter
Always the sound of late rain
Cut and rightfully falling
Into your cupped writing hand

Sighing, *goodbye, everybody*
Before taking that last drink

Becoming both albatross and anchor.

Her Measurements

It's been raining indoors for days.
There's a depression
beside her in the bed.

Raw fires once merged there.

Cold, she keeps her back turned now.
Sometimes she spins and looks—

hoping to find a body of water
to name after him.

Arable

Placing an ear to the endless ground,
she waits to hear the red peal
of the bells she tied to his feet,
before he was lowered into its loamy gut—
sewn inside that open emergency, where spacious
seconds were years, merging with shadow once feared.
Still silent, she listens for growth's breakage.

*   *   *   *   *   *

She takes the storm, open-eyed,
with her mouth, swallows
and waits for the music to swell
up from the depths of her body. –She knows it is there.
The sky they shared has already fallen
inside of her. –Now a blue newness is proofing.

Bottom Sustenance

You cleave to spleen
a humorless tumor on an organ
grinding away without a song
just vicissitudes of full and empty
fooling yourself eternally, internally

vent spleen with hard apple face
the waning light makes it look like
a fist or a storm

attempt to sharpen vision with spleen
spit black bile into eye
find blindness again

spleen as your own private black sea
captain of seizure and shipwreck
high on hubris and rum, sail on, sail on, sailor
into the low sulphurous gut of the kraken

or maybe just a turbid puddle
distorting reflections that skim its skin
a place for you to drown in the
hallowed shallows of yourself

the crabs wait for you to hit rock bottom
anxiously shuffling, sucking,
blowing bubbles in the muck
your eyes, lips, and tongue their fatty delicacies
all your splendid venom and heavy words lost on them.

Righteous Epic(ene)

anchor tattoo
wasted on skin
already stilled
by sailing hand

wizened fly paper

the lines laugh
from his face
from her face
it's your face

forget the
perfunctory kisses

echoes always delayed
measured in joy
quickly diminished

unsaid notes
hopeless poems
that puncture the air
with their whinging

Madame George
plays until
the record breaks

ballads bleed
sped up
saccharine show tunes

in needy blue flashes

of wee neon hours

needles of harsh light
numb the Liza Minnelli mask
comfortably worn

but the weightless lift
is running late

a shady operation

heels, eyelids,
thanksgiving chin,
dragging

you can't lean
into those shadows
for too long

that's when you fall

waving goodbye
with a nod
to the neighing mares
of your own youth
disowned

all this ash
and cigarette smoke

against the
cloying white diamond
off the atomizer

the walls swell

with welling nausea

in the three way mirror
everything is neatly
tucked away

but the sirens
down on the street
seem to say
you are hiding

your untamed brain
in the soft hell
between your legs

where development
is arrested

why so loud?

always a scream
never a whisper.

Measuring Cups

With her in a city
Where the newness
Goes to end

You are water
Seeking its own level

Sometimes just a trickle
While she's seemingly the sea

Measuring her moods
As you wade and weave
Through abrupt thermoclines

You dare not drink
Suppressing a thirst
Circumscribed by fire

Slowly you emerge
In some kind of dry birth
Tangled up in the jungle
Of her eyes

Dark, warm, familiar, nearly perfect

You collapse into her lap –
A lion without claw or fang

She feeds you sweets
Until you are blind
To the heated needlepoint message
Turning into frieze of Braille
On her left arm bridging over

Empty and diabetic
You want meat badly
Enough to tear at yourself

Too loyal to ever snap
At her feeding hand

For you know she
Could have gelded you
Back when this all began

Always scratching that itch
Just out of your own reach

Your roar expresses less
Than her whisper

She offers milk from breast
She offers honey from loin
Adds egg white and sugar from lip
Whips it into sweet cream

All fluff and peak

Like a good house pussycat
You lap it up with Cheshire smile
Pizzicato purr

She pats your head
Sets you down
To nap for hours

With wild moving dreams
Of hunter and hunted
Far removed

From watery domestic

Where the field
Is leveled in dusk's
Fleshy harvest

A late safari
Blood in distinguished crest
Free range

Here everything tastes
Strange and gamy

Deliciously new.

Actual Tigers

I just want another season,

says the wounded tiger
as he staggers back
to the place he first
found beauty

starving

seeking sustenance,
shade, mate

only to find paper
where meat used to be

poachers in the trees
blunderbusses aimed

he roars and hangs his fangs
shows glint of light from claws

the men find moon
as tiger strikes

beach red scream

a death dream of whale
swimming against current

dorsal fin ripped
into sweet oblivion

blood on sand
where bikinis used to be

that first taste of ocean
too strong and salty
to be forgotten

green and blue
in crest and crash
a strange change up

thank god
they saw it all
in colour once

tasted it on their tongues
almost mother, home

tiger licks wound
with ocean in each eye
rage, calm, rage again

waves could be horses
or guttered candles
with flames remounted

he stretches and yawns
knows their voices
as just a single playback

that misses everything
and says nothing
as it numbly roars.

The Stoker
for Karl Rossmann

bored over love
drunk and dancing
on the ship's deck in the rain
while dreams dryly rise
in the powder bowels of the hold

beyond the pallid light
found inside of me
is a fool's golden core
I'd surely pawn for liberty
and pursuit of bliss

the lady holds no flame
but rather a sword for me
the air seems low down
free in its pouring shadow
which hardly sharpens this light

parallax view of statue
shattered on stygian sea
drown me at her feet
if it brings ablution

bluely bloated on
tristesse of excess
too nauseous to wonder if
the slender-wristed translucent dollymop
remembers me as the stoker of her fire

she burns alive
in order to live
with the child inside

she yearns to scrape away

now treading the shoals
a fish relinquishing bowl

I found a new land
it makes me feel so
heartbroken and old

all these wide open spaces
still I'm claustrophobic
vomiting brave new vistas
standing cheap and feckless
in the splendid wreckage of my own shade

chaotic parades pass by
between highs of hallelujah
hang the low sober sounds
of long wars lost

most days my blood riots
in sonnets unfit to write
best to keep them down
crushed by the gut's rejection

here men are clapping machines
breaking down regularly
beneath glass ceilings always crashing
dull fragments caught in eye undazzled

there's no sanctity, sensitivity,
sympathy or sincerity here

streets snaking
with labyrinthine illogic

towards green lights
out of reach –

almost the hair, the eyes,
of my first lover
before it all turned red
in an infant second

rolled by two ugly drifters
they stabbed me from behind
without the courtesy of a sneer
for here in Amerika they only smile

now fat Brunelda rolls
her doughy body all over me
she stinks of yeast and miracles stillborn

her laugh is thunder
it rattles my bones
her sweat in pregnant pools
stagnates on my skin
then seeps in
and stains my soul

I read Ben Franklin to her
she falls fast asleep
it's all he's good for

I think of cool rivers
and dream of Oklahoma
as she dreams of me

I'm being carried towards a theater
lit up hot as harlot's blood
it seems more alive

than I can ever be

I find Amerika waiting there
with star staggered eyes
she's the last actress standing
on a stage covered in rotten fruit
heart long gone before I landed

she offers no pulse
for a buzzing fly
searching her slackened cavities
for whatever meat is left

her bed is flagstone unfurled
it finds me weak with hunger
collapsing in numb cataclysm
I find my name as scar across the face
I think of open fields waving goodbye

Amerika,

you once touched me from a distance
and dared me to follow you
I chased and caught a taste of your tongue
dipped my hands into your fire
felt up your great beautiful nothing
while your darkness swallowed me whole

then shat me out as the stranger
I should have stayed

burning alive to live
dying of thirst between seas.

How I Disappear
for Gregor S.

blues when sister plays her violin
I tremble and cling to the ceiling
naked, the hot bulb flickers with me

they shouldn't see me now

but the door opens
another wound

and it is familiar eyes
all over an unfamiliar me

mama faints,
papa curses,
throws apples

half crippled
I seek shelter

my ears
cannot stand
my voice

they shouldn't hear me now

when I say,
the next sunrise
shall be my last

my pride
spoiled milk
I've tried to swallow

this shell betrays
what rots inside

I've never been under
a heel this heavy before

tell sister
to breathe,
stretch her fingers –

each blessed one
a long white cat
in spot of sun

remember me
as scar
unafraid
of rain.

Just a Shadow

After birth altricial,
flight is tested.

She lifts her veil –
an apocalypse
honest blue and beautiful.

Pale bouquet becomes this
Ophelia rising from her stream.

A bright dream wrecked
by morning's darkness.

The feeding hand
she says tastes like ashes
is wholly her own.

The horses are hard rain in the stable.
She fixes a bath.

Another wobbling planet
mirrored in the water.
From a distance gentled.
Still close up the naked eye finds hunger –
a blind familiar savage, coldly encroaching.

She knows of a clearing where
the dog's tracks merge with those of the hunted –
just a flash, a flame of late sun on fading snow.
The arrow's immediacy is finally softened there.

She lays herself down in that minor place
beyond the blood dappled brambles,

safely finds herself a cord of wood –
a fire that burns itself alive to live.

The world is ending
in a way too human to believe.

Sudden night comes as burial above ground.
She closes her eyes to see.

The light aches to speak
in shadows long and lean
a language profoundly meaningless –
now the breath is gone.

The Noble Rise Above

the first time
Coltrane played Paris
the French booed
and threw copper centimes
at him

Coltrane just
closed his eyes
raw oceans gentling

and listened to
the sound of pennies
tapping the wood
of the stage

it reminded him
of rain falling down
onto the tin roof
of his first home

Coltrane mimicked
that sound with his horn
then quoted
Pennies from Heaven
for safe measure.

Love does migrate this way, more so during summer.
for Scott Wannberg

The last honest song and dance
Just left this tiny town
Turning the lights down and out
So that we may face the full moon
Before it howls itself away
Jackknifed like a sleeping dog
Time stops to look at herself
With eyes softer than before
The dust asks the cleaning lady
When the singer of songs is coming home
And will the sky be following him
You bet the birds are standing still
Barbed wild bunches on branches
Weighted with a feeling
Words would just disfigure
Only their open mouths swing with the wind
Freely welcoming ring of expressive silence
Royal and blue as the mountain
He stacked them in
So many musicians on fire
Inside of one king-sized heart
They are aching to play
Infinity Hootenanny says
Bring us your best soft shoe
The one man homecoming show
Will be an endless soiree
Of supreme sax blasts
And deft two-steps
Tapping out the Morse code of life
Transcribed on sheets of melody
Moving with the force of living water

That anybody can splash their face in
As they read this write of passage
In the moment
On fire with life
Wounds turning to wine
Before singing a song so human it hurts
One of many the maestro wrote
While riding the high country.

Country Bluebird Reimagined

she cradles a bluebird
in the palm of her
right hand,
hidden

she feels no need to
show it to you

to tell you
about the warmth
of its tiny belly

the way it rises and collapses
against her palm

it's an honest heartbeat,
an honest breath,
quickened by
the fear of human stain

simply an evergreen truth,
a sacred bond, unbroken

a poem that writes/rites/rights itself

if you could see her eyes
at this moment
you would understand
the soft surprise
of this sudden warmth

the way they see
far beyond

all of this
even while closing

if you could see her eyes
at this moment
you would understand
that the secret of flight
is revealed in life

in the light
she can only be
the source of

how else
could it weave
itself in and out of her
in the way that it does?
such a graceful lacing

how else
could it walk
both beside her
and inside of her
yet never falter,
never fade?

far beyond the bitter green hiss
of heat and frustration,
of small animal
caught in the canebrakes,
left for dead

where the music is always
composed in minor key
and the wind whips

up a familiar threnody
low and lonesome

there's an altar,
a limestone cathedral,
a tower and a bell ringing
urgent, wide open emergency

a plangent plea
for peace
in the valley
of her mind

still verdant,
still pure,
even in the slatternly
shadows of these spires

you see
it was always
her eyes
first

they told a story
even at half-moon

they elucidated
the secret of flight
same as life

spoke volumes
of the energy
in a bird's wing
when released

they held you
reflected you
when you were
at your most fragile

treasuring the touch
which, let's face it,
still is the purpose,
the point

never a word of dying
for she knows
it says nothing at all

of this bird
blue but unbroken
in the palm
of her hand
rising

without the
crushing weight
of surrender
or farewell.

Her blue ribbons, caught up in the breeze like that.
for Kimberly Schlagel

when she is away from me
I hold several pictures of her
in my mind
daguerreotypes captured in blood
sometimes a riot or sonnet
sometimes ballet on inner eyelid
deeply purpled by dream
a sudden quicksilver image
like her touch
it breathes auroras,
prismatic vistas,
and I'm warm, I swear.

when she returns to me
with skin softened
by lazy country days
and lavender oil
she'll read stories
from memory
faraway eyes
indexing frontiers
and I will listen
still as a sleeping horse
gentled by her hand,
her tender mercy –

a surrounding sun
a swallow of moon.

Photograph of Water

She was a fountain exquisitely lit from within.
A depth you could not fathom
but wanted to pass through,
testing with a finger first,
then gently easing hand before slipping in.
Watching her rise, fall, remake herself
over and over again.

Her music was Spring –

most things opening, some closing, birth bursting,
as old shadow wounds bled brighter sonnets
without cutting roses.

You were so young then. Impossible, it seems, now.

Eager to suspend motion,
its honest music, with a photograph –
content to touch her, yourself, from a distance.
You choose mirror over window; avoid eye contact
because the view reveals too much face to save.

Much older now –

watching her dry tongue twist,
arms bend back in this thalidomide way.
Even worse, her eyes popping
from crush of unseen impact.
As if shot from behind she jumps up with them
out of the chair you kicked away and dances for rain.

Felo de se

Mother felt the shot first,
one less heart kicking inside of her—

bones turning to glass
before the great breakage.

Rimy day,
yellow room,
this late sun has secret knowledge
of your wounds—

it throws the shadow
that carries you home.

Poppy face blown open,
down and flowing away
under distant bridge bending,
threatening tense touch—tubercular,

yet somehow golden,
like hers.

Her heavy hand

little bird
trapped indoors

*a dark omen
of death,*
said the girl

as she spilled
a few crumbs
from her heart
into a cupped hand

watching the bird disappear
then reappear again

wings making a papery sound
knocking over her fragile piggy knickknacks
before colliding against windowpane
against drop ceiling
panting and painted with pain

*so strange to see
a bird pant*

its open mouth
a bloody Mary
a budding misty rose
dripping slack beads
of a rosary disowned

shades of bruise
heliotrope and puce

little bird
not unlike sad but
pretty words
of poems
knowing no frontier

hiding for a while
trying to find
a place of rest

a few seconds of something
like nest
like home

a grounded broken thing
with volant dreams of repair

she found the bird
behind the vanity
in the bedroom
lured him out
with crumby hand
and snatched him

the bird grunted
then groaned
his bones
lighter than
the air in the room

hand closing
bird squawking
snap of neck
pop of eye

sounds so far removed
from the music
that little bird knew

remembering the place
he first found rest
for an eternal second
before the great fade

she looked away
as she dropped him
music-less
down into the
rubbish bin

and slammed
the story closed

never once catching
her own reflection
in the snapping
stainless steel lid.

Specific Gravity

curious bird
the yellow-billed Oxpecker
precariously saddling
the immense back
of the ill-tempered Hippo

she spends most of her life there
hardly a pretty bird
unable to warble when she
finally does fly

dependent on the mighty Hippo
all the sustenance its body yields

picking at old wounds
picking at the parasites
and fat auburn ticks
that look oddly Roman

the Hippo serves a purpose
and some forget
that he is widely regarded
as one of land's most dangerous mammals
especially when one foolishly attempts
a surprise attack

the Hippo can outrun any
praying human, predator, or parasite
without breaking a blood sweat

so count your little blessings
when he tastefully decides
to stop and settle for a midday

graze in the lush grass
as to avoid indigestion

constructive aggression

the yellow-billed Oxpecker
supposedly serves a purpose too,
but her beak is dull
and often untrue in its
myopic aim

she short eyes the prize
she picks at a wound
and poisons only herself
she dies and no one notices
not the Hippo, or even the wound,
for she too was a parasite

the parasite serves no purpose
a profoundly meaningless existence
the only significant act of its life
is leaving it
its only form of expression is sucking
for without the sucking
it is already dead
it depends on a host
for life, shape, and uneasy,
insincere validation

the Hippo hardly even notices
any of this
he soulfully yawns
and when he does
you are reminded
of a cobra striking

as it pauses actual air
then pushes it again

as he moves on
toward the cool rivers
he often dreams of

huge heart too light
to be a burden
too alive
to be a legend

hardly holy
for that is an empty word
only a self-righteous human
would ascribe to a being

he knows of much
better uses for mud

even when it dumbly
spells itself backwards
if only for self-definition –
self-dissolution.

It doesn't take a professor.

Aside
from
the
obvious,

what's
the
difference
between
a
living
writer
and
a
dead
writer?

The dead one cannot improve.

Pantry Pride

Chick McLittle is a Humpty Dumpty manchild
with a Holden Caulfield complex,
and a big fat golden hen
of a woman that he calls Mama Honey Cutlet.

He's forever falling with
that phony blue sky he can't stand.
He's always cracking in the same shell shamelessly.

Every time he hears that old red-eyed rooster
murder another morning with its bloody scream
he cries for his sweet mama, the first of many bottles
he'll need to make it through another day on the farm.

She comes and coos, pats his balding head,
ever sensitive to the soft spot;
picks him up and coddles him as she would an egg,
lets him sup at her warm nipple a little,
sweetly swaddles her elongated infant
in succulent measures of marinated flesh;

until the best part of him runs wild,
scrambles a marathon of yellow ribbons racing
down her meaty strip of leg,
past the spatchcocked place
where the loud roving swine sniff out truffles,

towards the finish line where be-goitered local yokels
yuk it up, play pinochle, toss horseshoes,
and wait for another late breakfast
to be served out in the barnyard.

Mama Honey Cutlet waves an open flame,

a winner's flag for her forever worried little egg man;
he'll throw a deviled tantrum if he's not the first to eat.

She's an excitable woman
sweating beads of sweet peas
and buttery pearls of onion,
biscuit gravy and bacon fat
sizzling with the sun.

Wind raises her checkered dress
as his insatiable sausage snout finds its way
back to the all you can eat buffet her folds offer.
A place where he becomes champion,
then glutton, then sleepy little baby.

She burps him first, changes his feculent diaper,
then cuts a cold steak from her shoulder,
unfolds it into a blindfold for his raw eyes
blackened by lack of sleep.

She sings him into slumber with a golden lullaby
only pure and honest to his own ear.
He starts snoring up a storm.
She finds the eye, big and stupid
as a stunned chicken's,

she sees herself reflected in it
and looks away,
swallows her pride,
tastes him again.

The silo pours its shadow
into all the empty bottles
and other things
he drained and discarded.

On the fence
the rooster watches
and knows to keep
its big mouth shut.

Outlaw Banking

The west has been tamed beyond recognition.
The sun is mightily confused.

Cowpokes second as stagehands.
Morning ragged as they rig clouds with wheels.
Rolling them down into brown, ugly town
with modest thunder mistook for applause.
Fitting roadrunner for brakes, planting tumbleweed,
doctoring frontiers—all horses neutral
—where is the wind?

Mystical whistle—dry saloon—crisp women crumble,
the smell of something chicken fried.
Here the man in black hides;
takes an early shift as bank teller,
exchanges myths with the compact populace.
Last night the bottle let him down.

Old Bart is the only moustache left.
Bleary-eyed, he follows the carrion birds blindly—
see, the raised braille connects everything.
Chasing the horizon, Bart shouts, WATER!
The rest drop duty and follow—
jagged spurs in full jangle.
Eager to load their pistols, take ten paces,
turn and aim for the heart of the sun—blank faces, all.

Suddenly, it is night—no coyotes—
moon, of course.

Frontier Doctored

when neighing mares grow sick of motion
cease loping across her half-mooned eyes

I send my mind with hers
out into the clearing
which, even in this late light,
is the color of good white wine

and there is a gentling
that this indigo gloaming brings
a fathomless depth and range
a new language, a softer tongue
reads the runes of this sublimation hour

her stillness tells me
she has found the place
where she first knew rest

her eyes not closed
but inward and dreaming

I turn mine back too
wind the clock
cross the threshold
and pursue her
new hypnotic

not a mirror wet with breath
or a scar turned phantom with rain

just an ancient, unmapped
red rock mesa
a fire escape winding

up toward a sky
not quite ready
for this predicate challenge

our calm but certain
need to push proof
and conclusion
out of that tall, storied window

this bankrupt myth
that is the horizon

pale and blue as the corners
we once painted ourselves into
before buying our brilliant eyes
back from the birds we followed blindly

not knowing they knew better
despite their dissuasive songs

you see,
blackbirds never say
goodbye

a lesson measured in salt
mistook for sugar
an infant baker

his pie should be a metaphor
for what?
I do not know

and now it's finally our time,
our turn, turn, turn,
to doctor this frontier

half-smiling,
half-knowing,
it will just hurt a bit.

Potatoes

Charlie Rich was speaking
directly to him from the flooding guts
of the cheap stereo he loved so much.
A silver-white leviathan rising, saying,
it seems silly to sing a blues sober.
He agreed. Approached and took
a knee. Washed his hands in
that muddy water. Bottled it
and sold it to himself as vodka.
Deep, strong pulls—a good burn—
the last thing he'd remember.

He was moving south
on a greyhound—no, a train—
the bells told him so.
Half of his face pressed
against the window glass
night was turning into mirror.
The cool side of the moon.
He felt more open than empty.
The darkness finally seemed grand.
So he rested his light, and traveled.

It wasn't recidivism that found him
brushing the chilly bathroom floor from his face.
Man, he wanted to drink that floor,
before it iced over and the careless
skate blades bled him.
Someplace close by somebody was burning homefries.
He retched and saw dry dwarf stars.
She was dancing around him—
almost 40 years and those legs were still twin prizes.
The spiders had left them alone—

wild horse and shotgun.
He felt scooped out inside,
hollow as those poems he'd been reading.
He wished she had a vice.
Then they could rot together, grow extra eyes,
not miss a thing.
She said, *goodbye,* closed the door, and went to work.
Rushed footsteps fading, tap-tapping out
that lonesome tune, too honest.

Head On

I met Smokin' Joe Frazier
at target market in Port Richmond
a year or so before he moved on.
He was buying a flat screen TV,
said he was going to donate it to the local
Police Athletic League.

I called him the Champ,
told him he was the best boxer that ever lived.
He gave me a surprised look and said,
"nah, Ali was, I was the best fighter."

When I went to shake his hand, he just shook his head,
held out his fists – taped, gloved,
and broken so many times
they resembled tight fossilized storms,
petrified ambuscades.
He could barely open them without grimacing in pain.

He stared me down with cagey eyes
for an animal minute,
then grunted and gave me a pound with the left one –
the same fist that knocked out 27 chumps;
that hook belonged in a museum or an abattoir –

I flinched a little, he shadowed a flurry,
caught me mid-dodge and feint,
said, "thanks kid, you've got heart;
use your neck less, tuck in that chin."

He turned and walked away.
Only one other person even recognized him.

I pictured him walking through all those flagrant blows,
head on, still standing, always moving forward –
a face in the fire, fierce and fearless.
No dancing, no prancing,
just pure puncher's advantage.

No words, for action is enough.
Butterflies and bees are sweet,
but the raw poetry of the simple man
swears by something more immediate –

knows the Champ always fights himself first.

Beguilement (or what Klaus said to the Butterfly)

at first
you were
a sweet irritation
to me,

butterfly

filament thin wings
their papery sound

a flutter of
almost fleshy
nothingness

drawn to me
as tongue is
to bad tooth

why are you
so unafraid?

is it the wind
that makes you shiver
like this,

or just the
shock of contact,

butterfly?

so many have seen

this net of darkness
pouring from my eyes
in torrent, in tear,

collecting in
reflective pools
pregnant and still

so few
have delved
below
the surface

investigated the
enlarged heart,
lent an ear to
the simple song
that beats beneath –

a restless rhythm
of survival

pain
in bubbles
rising
only to burst

what have you seen,
what have you heard,

butterfly?

can it be
my eyes –

sometimes twin tyrants raging,
other times tapped hydrants
freely flowing

a confluence of summer colors:
cooling children
leaping, and loping,
laughing through
sudden rainbow,
softly shot –

have these old tired eyes
become a light source
for you,
only you,

butterfly?

have you sent your
milky infant eyes
with all their warmth
past this mask I wear,
this flash frozen façade,

to a place where
the ice is
finally melting
in seismic drip?

am I both flower,
and flame,
to you,

butterfly?

my throbbing palm,
closed in an instant,
could disrupt
your graceful arc,
endanger your
empyreal (f)light,
with the weighted crush
of calculated impact,

butterfly

a final metamorphosis,
or maybe
just a
dreamless sleep

awaits with
a killing stillness

an unbending end
to this
beguilement

the easy music
and sweetly
confusing amusement
we now share

here where the light
is soft and strong

does it not
seem brighter now,

butterfly?

prismatic wings
unfolding smile

this odd gentling
this curious metamorphosis

I feel my blood
turning into ballet

I am a child again.

Nearly a Morning
for Frances Farmer

cinema usherette
leads herself down
to the screen

the sloping floor
a beach stretching
out to sea

she projects herself
high as star uncharted
trembling in every lens

she's protected now
preserved on celluloid

she steals the highlights,
makes you reel

a blonde balm so close
to your burning palms

look don't touch
her eyes devour you

she delivers the lines
with hungry archer urgency
with wild animal honesty

a hunter/hunted climate

the soft hells and heavens of her impact
drain the chambers of your heart

the beat goes on
until the breath is gone

burgundy curtain closes
crushed velvet bleeds
the end brings sorrow

she tells you it's ok,
god is dead

the scene changes

you follow her car
through blackout zones

her headlights
project the road

beacon dimmed
senses dulled

there is a war inside
a rush and a push
of blood

she drinks bourbon
straight from the bottle

lit cigarette dangles
the way you wish to
from her mouth

a white hot conversation

would you take her hand, flaming

and scale the walls?

better yet,
would you tear them down for her?

hold her hair back when she's sick
of the nauseous green windows
the free exteriors they distort

the faceless fail to erase her
with ice bath, electric shock,
thorazine, broken promises,

forced sodomy and lobotomy
is no direction home

prism
prison
pinwheel
pincushion

touch her now

trace her narrow body
with stick of chalk
she once dropped in class

embrace her with soft white outline
until she becomes a garden

and the rain chooses her humble thirst
while the rest burn in their arrogance

she blooms
they wither

this late rising
nearly a morning.

Watercolour of a Lighthouse

Then…

Ocean Beach

she let me walk beside her
stones in both pockets
replacing miracles

I did not know

her brow soft as anything
slate sky and swallowing squall
light still between our skin
the privilege of dreams

sand against eye
turning to ash in throat
the oppressive choke
we could not digest
we could not announce

surf as song
key all wrong
still seagull
knew her name

her mouth
a fault line
my lips
waltzed upon

her eyes
an unsheltered storm

touching all the things
my eyes could only see

as they left her
for a moment
then returned
and she was gone

another way
to find blindness.

*   *   *

Yesterday…

Ocean Beach

alone

with two stones
in my pocket

seagulls still
screeching her name
it's sad

the sea's spray
salt in wound
that time
wants no part of

it would
only be
to my detriment
if I tried to

explain this

with words
that served
to disfigure
the infinite eight
we created

lonely broken
zeros now.

*   *   *

Present...

Fuck this
I'll say it
she was
my own
personal tsunami
the Charlie Sheen
I wanted to save

my cradle
my grave

she tried
I tried
we tired.

Blood on Blood

They're going to ask you
questions about the rescue reflex,
and how you slept through
the telephone's vehement night ringing.

About the boy,
his eyes in that video,
bruises wide as seas,
tugging, turning blue to gray –

a civil war,
a traitor's winter

– split yet fixed on something
freely sliding past the frame.

The way he spoke of six-sided
snowflakes and vague space
inside seconds passing –
said, *"silence is made,
not found, in earnest."*

The purple poetry of birds
with wings not beating
outside the window
on the tense wire
weighted low by rain.

*Why did he write about them?
Why did he call them his friends?*

And you'll tell them
about that gorgeous morning

the two of you walked down to the beach
while the rest slept off ruined nerves
on tangled beds, at the mercy of alarms.

You said,
"can you smell the jasmine?"
He said,
*"I thought it was you,
your skin, your shampoo, mother."*

A rare smile from the boy,
so quick and sincere.
You paused, felt new.
Lost your pace, fell behind.

Waving back, he screamed,
"hurry, the sand misses our footprints!"

The moon still pinned in depth of sky,
the slumberous sun housed in his eyes,

the ocean roaring
as the waves rode in
on the backs of actual tigers.

He was growing in the distance
while you diminished –

a severed cord,
the letting go

– not empty,
just open.

Staircase Wit
for Theresa Duncan & Jeremy Blake

1. Tenebrous Tango

lungs black and crumpled
old accordions she pawned
for two big bright coins
to place over each eye
in an effort to sleep
to shield them from theft

indigo insomnia
"the moon is in my blood,"
she would say,
"my mood is on a trapeze"

she always lost her breath
during the late night monologues
as we burned together
at opposite poles
of the same bed.

2. Epic Soundtrack

*Chet Baker, Mabel Mercer,
Tindersticks, Neko Case,*

what she called the
*out of the blue
epic soundtrack*

an old black & white romance
turning to snow
on the shiftless

muted tube

a vase of forget-me-nots
effaced by the smoke
she created in chain succession
choking beside the rising ashtray

down her narrow gullet
vodka lime unbridled
pills spilled, secrets surrendered.

3. Leaving Song

shadow spent
she returned to bed
silhouetted in light
parched and ghost pale
a whispering apparition

so quiet when she finally slept
that I had to check for a breath
place my ear to her breast
hoping to hear her song,
any song, except for
one of leaving

a perplexing knot
tight lightning
thunderous
oblivion train
rattling her rail
thin bones
a dancer's body
once weightless.

4. Bibliophobia

rows of books domino
analphabetic
answerless
dust
untouched
sullen
silent
slow life
turning still
she's been gone
three years today
Kafka spread-eagled
Plath dog-eared
I can't read
them anymore
they can't touch me
the way she did
with a poem
from her own hand.

5. Fuzz on Prism

Theresa,

would you believe
it didn't even rain
that day you
said goodbye?

I had a response
not perfect
but sincere

I once shared it
with you in a dream

strained it through
a fuzzy prism

made it
a moving picture

you just shook
your head

a spectacular flash
of wild honey highlight
offset by deep dusky root

smiled soft serve sarcasm
eyes bright wonder
eyes sharp spleen

and said,

*"spare me the wit
of your staircase."*

6. Rain on Lens

shattered tableau
channeled
projected
through child's
smarting eyes

salt as cauterant
for wound

it's here wonder
limps away

it's here
newness ends

the music
sounds ruined

fall into something
fall into someone

the sea calls to me
tells me it's still her
draws me in

the depths reveal
she wasn't lying

my last thought
her lasting breath.

Blepharospasm

no worries Eric Roberts

we have all chased our Star 80
if only with our minds

at least I think we have

the way she catches the eye first
then snatches it
when you aren't looking

uses it as an olive
in her stirred martini
to take away the shakes

only to return
fresh and coquettish
with it preserved
in a pickling jar

stick it back in
to the dry, raw,
blood-black socket

with delicate
exacting hand

and you want to touch her
reciprocate this sudden tenderness

but she's just too perfect
and you feel like a disturbance
as you watch her undress

touch herself
in feathery strokes
put on a show for you

so you leave the room
seared by skid row neon,

her flashpoint physiognomy
scorches torrid shroud
over your retina

gift turns to curse
as guilt has its way

it manifests as a restless twitch
a ragged spasm in one eye
then moves on to the other

and you'd like a straight razor
to slice open the void
in hopes that it drips
one vision pure

or just a sterile spoon
to scoop it out forever

for it drives you crazy
and that's a day trip

you see,
there are some dark kingdoms
where a one-eyed man can still make it

some selfless buzzing maidens waiting
autumn butterflies drowned in wine

or maybe just death's head moths
too close to the flame

not quite beauties
but alright,
from the right angle,
in the right light

they swallow
their glasses of chablis
and start to sparkle

they belch and
form a chorus

sing,
"Cyclops, we want you."

it's hardly sincere
that flatulent noise

but if you let it
it can sound like heaven
after eleven

it can fix
things for
a little while

gauze the wound
itching to be wild

until the morning
wrecks it all
again

with anxious light
and terrible secrets

opening
with graceful carelessness

macabre dances
on the air.

Anatomy of Egg

1. Chalaza

red sparkling life

the lover's lips
first seen
as wings
spread across
the pulpy sky
of your mother's womb

you waited
just a lifetime
to recreate
this severed cord

a wound opening

sucking on your thumb.

* * *

2. Yolk

heart refuse
to become golden

remain
raw and bloody

for only then
do you serve

your function.

* * *

3. Vitelline

Dahlia your smile
is my scar

as you sleep
swaddled
by yolky sun

both eyes
wide open

expression
naked
forever.

* * *

4. Albumen

I reach for
your highest shoulder

a weathered pyramid
puncturing the firmament

a dusky beak
cracking the shell

the moon
finds itself

as a bruise
weighing down
your right eyelid

forming daguerreotypes
of puce and silver
beneath filament thin
white skin

quick to fade
as I shake
you awake

a tiny star
trembling

falling
on my tongue

you taste
like wine
and iron

blood
spilled
into
milk.

Sunspots
for Katarina

she told me
that she first felt
the cancer inside of her
when she laughed

she said the tumors
looked like
sunspots when x-rayed

when I heard that
I felt a breakage
all the way down
deep inside

yet somehow
her eyes
still smiled

when we kissed
I could taste
her sickness

one night
I commented
on her naked body
while we were
making love

I said,
"even your scars
seem luminous
to my eyes"

she thought
I said stars

it was true,
you know

I could have
looked at her
for 500 more years

and every time
she'd still seem new
to me

I've kept the cassette tape
she gave me
for my 17th birthday

weightless recordings
of Katarina playing violin
for a roomful of family
and their friends
when she was just a child

young lithe fingers
a deft ballet across
the slender neck
of that sad, old instrument

the music never cries
it simply says,
I'm alive

the tape is worn thin
it hisses now

not like a snake
but rather
an easy zephyr
through the trees
when they are full

I keep an old cassette deck
out in my van

sometimes
I just drive in circles
around the neighborhood
where she lived

and listen to what
she has to say

as she breaks
to be beautiful

as her grace
disrupts the disorder
of my day.

Neural Piano
for Grace Paynter

You see,

her mind was never
confined to that room

sea foam soothing green
gall bladder attacks
and projectile vomit

no,

it moved with music
scales sliding sideways
was scented
all things vernal

she sent it beyond
that jonquil window

where the sunlight
was weaker than
the pale blue
flame of her eyes

entire bouquets
used to bloom there

out into the garden
where the beauty
was so exquisite
it was maddening

the wires, drips,
patches, and i.v.
simply ceased to be

enforced reality no longer
her sterile misericorde
the aim always a blank point

bored in the way
of the boring
she suffered graciously

after they cracked
her treasured chest

the doctors
disinterred songs
classic harmonies
conducted by
dusk's steely hand

*"show me the way
from sin to mercy*

I'm your sister's sister,"

she said to me

then she pointed
at a pint of blood
cooling on a hook

screamed,

*"it's not a cardinal,
you fool!*

it's a coppery-tailed trogon"

the breast inflamed,
the breast infected,

redder than hers

she convinced me
it was perched
on a hibiscus

her tongue swollen,
her breath infernal,
Wesleyan,

yet almost sweet
real and regal
to me

her bare legs
still long, aristocratic,

translucent carriages,

she said,

*"these birds
are attached
with sensitive wires
to my nerves"*

as her unplugged eyes
rained down cadenzas

as her tears
turned to jewelry

brightly flooding
the room she never knew

with a light, her light,
which seemed to say,

*"what's so damn lucky
about that sun

if it can't touch me,
walk beside me anymore?"*

it was there
in that present

that her wounds
feminine as Christ's

bled truth

drip drop dripped

off of ivory towers
into the ebony void

where my eyes
worked with insect agony

to reconcile a locked scene
that ached for a piano,

a minor key
for a kingdom
of rain.

Cancel Stars

1.

gypsy thrush

she rinses the stillness –

which reminds her of
cornered hobby horse

a diminishing static
best expressed by silence

and soft, slumberous
ponies, in pain
dreading rides –

with gaping yawns
and gypsy ukulele

in her eyes
nesting thrushes
speckled clutches
gently cupped
in shape of dream

walking away
a full, round pain
descending into song

she is no frozen rose
clipped by perfect teeth
aching with the deep empty,
the early empathy,

of motion created
just to suspend itself

some premature destiny,
some absent creation,

the true aim
corrupted by
sudden awakening

a rather
late flower
blooming;
fiery saxophone bell,
all limpid melody,
blowing

with notes out of the blue
against the black relief
of all colors at once

grievously colliding
into a brighter nowhere

her father's hands,
callous,

after the war
touching her

inside some sudden night
their softness gone
too hard to be his
yet they are

all over.

2.

lambent lamb

appropriate light
surrounds her
now

little lambent lamb
grazing a green
too true to know

her eyes meet
yours with questions,
with coyotes crossing

and sharp,
lacerating beauty

surprised,

all too soon,
numbed

she hates
when the
heat outside rises
higher than
the temperature
of the blood
inside her own body

late garden parties,
4th of July,
the marinated smiles
of overfriendly uncles

the alcoholic topography
of their oily skin;
a vessel bursting
in vain

swimming in her pool
underwater viewing

the lights are ghosts
all alone and floating,
almost friendly

the sky seems
to separate
into a revelation

quickly forgotten

the blood burns
as it rushes downward
spiraling from thigh
sadly dripping
sticky sickness

fireworks exploding
hot, bright, beautiful,
and stupid

are they really
so distant?

could they be stars
accepting these wishes
graciously?

or is it
just breath
soured by whiskey
canceling it all
in a disastrous mash?

oh, maybe it's
one in the same

after all

in part
and in whole

the slow, burning details;
an incautious sun rising,
wounding the face of the sky

from a static horizon
best not remembered

moving away
in uncertain
circling agony

yes,
she sees
it all

and
it hurts

the stars
trembling blue
and vanishing

blank,
when she remembers.

May Day

With the first burst of siren—

A flashing sound of red and blue
merging into wide purple emergency –
a circular bruise of anti-sun lurching

—The hounds joined in.
Barking their knives before
the children received their blooding.

Freshly skinned initiates for a ceremony so old.

The fox was weary but focused,
moving through the coverts
and brambles without frenzy.
Senses ignited, warding off the fear
that this was a hunt not a chase.

He saw a hare leaping and loping in the clearing.
Today he'd bring her no harm.

He remembered the time he gored one,
dipped his swift paws into the slow dazzling guts
of that noble-eyed creature as she shuddered
and drew her last breath.

No joy in his marrow as he ran scarlet circles
around the hoary trunk of a birch.

Fox was not a destroyer.
He did this just to trick the men and their dogs.

Fox heard the sound of water rushing,
expected to see the cool river mirroring
the sky's everything-blank-everything again expression.
But it was just the fierce footfalls of
red-coated horsemen tracking him.

He could smell meat from past game hunts
rotting between their teeth. Time was closing in.

The leaves in the trees
pressed themselves into death masks,
gravely whispered, *it's getting late.*

Fox felt it before it was heard.
His breath was shallow,
his heart left his chest with every beat.

There was a weighted shadow over him
much greater than he ever could be.
He collapsed in elegant surrender,
only to rise up from his body.

The hounds went quiet in the killing stillness
of that stolen moment.
Somehow rinsed away, maybe retreating.

Fox looked down and saw the hare he spared,
became dizzy and started to fall.
There was no fear, he sensed the connection,
her eyes pouring a net of light, a healing cradle
for his broken body.

He tasted her breath.
Felt his lungs open
in harmony with his heart.

She was his place of rest.

In the Depths of Something Good

Mama cut her tongue loose
while the frame lost its edges
in that balmy harbor bar.

Clyfford held his own,
knew it was sometimes best to just listen
when a woman was speaking.

She was drunk and talking about the day of his birth.
The womb couldn't be abstracted in this forum.
Though the form was hardly concrete either.

You didn't want out of there, she said,
before ordering another sherry.

Clyfford thought of his knifed palette,
the guts beneath his bloodied canvas—
flash bruise of color, texture, and image
fused into raw living spirit.

Human brushing divine.
Jungle fires in reverse.
The deep blue toll of harbor bells.
A new language. Sailors singing salty shanties
of strumpets, sirens, and shipwrecks; torn sky of oil.

It had been raining hard bop jazz all day, she said,
while flagging the waitress for more sherry.

Clyfford thought of a deep red umbrella
but it was more a sound than an object—
luscious wind going wild
in a tree he wished to climb.

Patience dripped its port wine stain
down onto his high forehead.
He supposed that's where he first learned it.
Virtuous patience, as the folks say.
Nine months of training.

Outside the old pier was creaking
as old piers are wont to.

You didn't even cry when you arrived.
The doctor said boy's about as animated as Rushmore.
She just kept on going, with her recurring sherry,
her fistful of ugly oyster crackers dipped in horseradish.

He loved her for it.
He laughed with his eyes.
It felt better that way.

Later he'd paint her,
all of her,
scent, sight, sound, spittle spray,
the whole human.

He doubted she'd even recognize herself.
But he knew he'd find himself
as a child again inside of her.

*Found, lost, found again
in the depths of something good.*

He said that to himself.
He sounded like his mother.

Acknowledgements & Permissions

Medallion level: Kimberly Schlagel, Buster McNutley, Mama Sass, Soul Sister Sookie, Tim Buck, Apryl Skies, Alicia Winski, Maria Gornell, Lynne Hayes, Karen Bowles, Marlene Lennon, Hank Beukema, Cynthia Terese Scott, Ness Bloo, Danny Bejar, D.C. Berman, Will Oldham, Bill Callahan, and The Popcorn Park Zoo.

Especial gratitude to the editors of the following publications where some of these poems were first printed: Calliope Nerve, The Criterion, Triggerfish Critical Review, Leaf Garden Press, Durable Goods, Take It to the Street Poetry Review, Edgar & Lenore's Publishing House – Edgar Allan Poet, Virgogray Press, Montucky Review, and Alligator Stew – Pig Ear Press.

Cover photograph: Halloween – 1964 by Grace Paynter

Cover models: Joanne Crawford & Marie "Cookie" Ford

Cover text, treatments, and pumpkin bread: Mark Stetsko

About the Author

Photo by Joanne Crawford

William Crawford has authored one other collection of poems entitled, *Fire in the Marrow (NeoPoiesis Press).* His writing has been twice nominated for the Pushcart Prize. His work has been published globally in numerous magazines and anthologies. Currently, his poetry is being translated into Polish. William abides in Philadelphia, Pennsylvania, and is an animal rights activist.

www.ingramcontent.com/pod-product-compliance
Lightning Source LLC
Chambersburg PA
CBHW032129090426
42743CB00007B/523